Daughters of Leda

By

Lee Pennington

DAUGHTERS OF LEDA

Published by Winchester Cottage Print

In Louisville, KY

Printed by LSI, Nashville, TN

U.S.A.

Cover and design by Jill Baker

Illustrated by Jill Baker

Printed in the United States of America

March 2017

First Edition

“A shudder in the loins engenders there
The broken wall, the burning roof and tower…
So mastered by the brute blood of the air,
Did she put on his knowledge with his power”

From *Leda and the Swan*--W. B. Yeats

Table of Contents

ILLUSTRATIONS BY JILL BAKER

Dedication

For Leda, half goddess/half mortal,

and all her children

Lee Pennington

EARTH

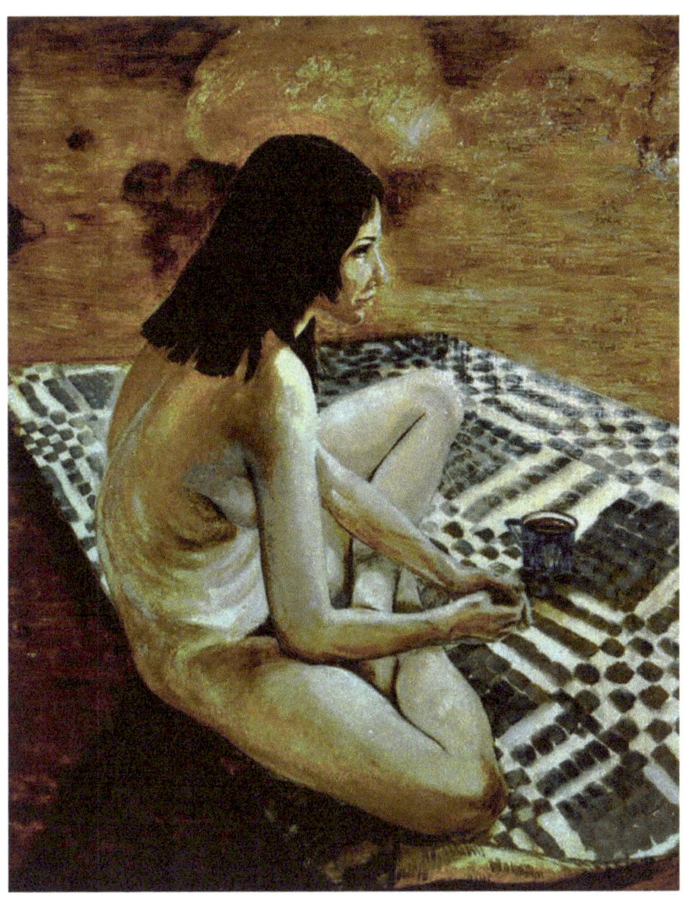

A WOMAN'S GLORY

when I touch your hair I hold earth
webs entanglement
love born suddenly as smoke
rivers dance on stones
wind hair around my face
caught life in dew
sun sparkles over meadows
when your hair falls
over thoughts and me
big clouds swirl in time
I cannot comprehend
the fire in your eyes
glass mirrors for my sanity
I kiss where kisses all should be
hunting out the source
of life and love
something like warm edges
of dreams spilling light
your glory your gift
into precious darkness

CANOPY

Thinking V though not spoken fear
not yet gone umbrella thoughts rise
where candle canopy leaves hold
morning light--dance of sorts.

A fuzzy squirrel walks length of limb
plunges across open dream
clear as wind
shatters an orchestral explosion
falling dew down at end of leaves.

It is this way the great V
open feminine legs
holding love eternity.

Old in willingness of want
as if darkness were color true
as if old passions could hide here
in warm hearts of wonder
holy moment profane.

ALTHOUGH YOU MAY NOT KNOW

Although you may not know I stand beside you now
my eyes float across your form knowing beauty well
you hold strange feminine deeply light exploding yes
shattering all everything as night begins to swell

you are sunny lips of dawn warm on rising wind
hips tall grass swaying dancing even as your hair
I am captured by your heat this great field blowing
awakened wet floating first on clouds now on air

let distance be no reason nor time tear us apart
we are here we are there where we briefly stand
near dreams near thoughts near hope near hearts
awakened we rise walk and wake love and land

no choice now but be ourselves always we will be
neither time place nor present birds roaming wing
we search feathers dropped perhaps purposely placed
around souls together bound by songs we sing

BEAUTY

Close your eyes and see yourself.
Then look in mirror and see yourself again.
Stand there unencumbered sense yourself.
Notice there is beauty all over you.
Notice there is beauty inside of you.
Notice there is beauty all around you.
It is your aura.
It is your skin that holds your beauty in.
Notice that you walk in beauty and are yourself the ground you walk.
Wrap your arms around yourself.
For a moment hold your beauty sense its glow.
Now go and meet the day beauty spilling from you beauty dripping from your wings.
Fly beauty fly.

GARDEN

The sun filters through rain come May
past distant trains past birds
caught in love on the wing
past mourning doves awake from willing night
birthing bubble sounds wrecking quiet.

The wind unmarried now walks in wet shoes
across unstable green shaking away
mirror orbs prisms for a million earths
baptizing roots with Jesus juice.

Two holy wrens toward cardinal points
draw crucifix across the sky.
Sweet shrub sanctifies the air.
Haloed in paradises last night
the serpent flower moon
slithers dark horizon below trees.

IN AND OUT

when I am in I want always to be
when I am out I want always back again
when you are in I want you always to be
when you are out I want you always back again

MILKWOOD'S EDGE

I have stood near silent at milkwoods edge
felt wind tug me and them
tiny gray love gifts life with wings
scatter fly a million ways
dance breath of feathers
tumble turn seek mating place
with earth.

I myself have
been that same gray fuzz
silently lifting skirts
my seed sailing up and up
my own fairy angel wings
swirling cotton candy love
till dropping again to earth.

THERE ARE NO WALLS

There are no walls to hold your thoughts there are no bars to bind your dreams.
The sun falls equally on everyone and water fills all streams.
Wind knows no bounds of love no more than earth's silent call
Where trees reach in autumn quest and golden leaves fall.
The earth's a silent lonely place if your eyes fail to see
Beauty just to kiss your face bent on folded knee.
You cannot claim night your own some special sorrow
Today's brief moment is just a wink flirting with tomorrow.

DIRT STONES SPEAK

dirt stones speak roots underfoot
breathing things feet wonderment
dark worm prints light silver trial
moon breath along silent sand

wind a handmaiden for such light
fingers among branches touch
some great silence into song
down below edge of your smile

now in clouds a great sun comes
wakes willingly the wonder world
shares music of red skies
bound to whispering of our eyes

splashing river new to this terrain
sound so precious it promises rain
know this torture too shall pass
when eagles fly again in pain

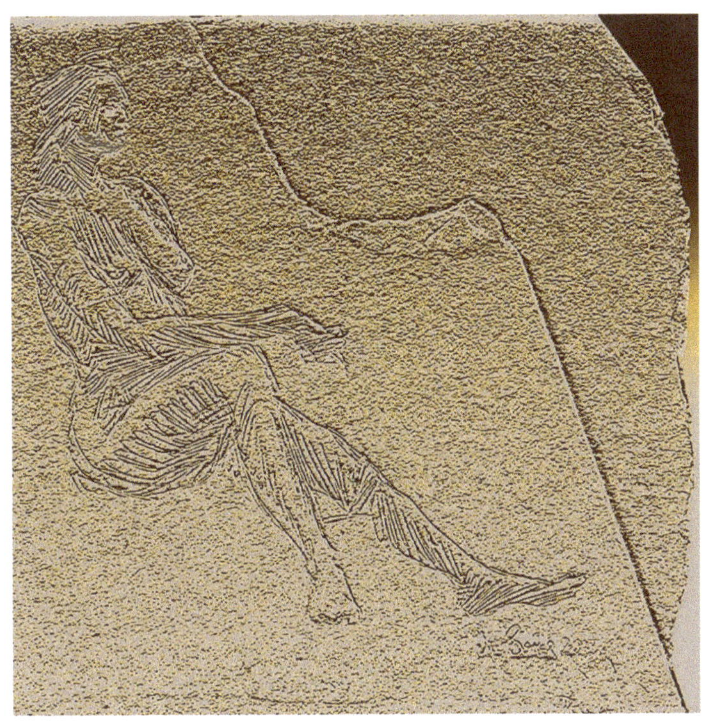

Dirt Stones Speak

INSIDE YOUR DARK

Inside you light licks dark
no force control or hold back
moments turned flesh then
upward burn color of gold

breath confine silver
opens your rise to sing
wrens mimic thrush complain
whippoorwills wake spring

wild rivers run embrace
holy web thought and bliss
pale wind bends your roots water
splashes stone shadows miss

you press all to your breast
drums talk worth and take
light spills brightly over all your skin
inside love screams birth and wake

SPECIAL

How do I tell you?
You are more special
than even your dreams
can tell and they don't lie.
You are woman
holy feminine carrier of life
bearer of wonder and mystery
a smile that trees bow down to.
Your form wrapped in love arms
universe delight artist's light
poet's muse smoke rising to gods
sage smoke words talk words.
Your lips blurred moonlight
you are hair woman's hair.
Bright around dark enigma.
Fingers that know touch
that reach hold caress
you step gently between heartbeats.

feet gifted to earth's touch.
When you are near things tremble
even I held to your journey
by some special web.
How do I tell you?
Special love gifted
the poet the poem
the singer the song
the dancer the dance
How do I tell you
held in your trance?

THE MUSE WON'T SLEEP

The muse won't sleep she pulls at me
 my heart dreads weight of dream
night and love. You stand nude
awake to rising sun aware of wind
soft as lips on your skin your feet
against morning grass soaking dew.

I picture of your voice
as it rides over a still water lake
even at a distance too far to hear
words come clear sounds embrace
thoughts as I hold them here.

So who are you except sun and wind
earth and rain? How does your voice
sweet come this way where two shadows
meet each wrap each dance and sway?

And how can I mere slave to words
love resist such morning whispers
mind restless with thoughts of us
two shadows tumbling now in grass?

TO HEAR YOUR VOICE

To hear your voice is to know the secret of clouds
Whispering as they do to wind at dawn trees
Lifting green fingers waving greetings of love.
To hear your voice is to know subtle rain
Bathing heart and senses beyond crystal dream
Listening to wake of lapping stream.
To hear your voice is to know hush of dirt
Where roots deep down find gift of earth
Life springs up near greening of our worth.
To hear your voice is to know whisper of sun
And wind dancing shadows across the lawn
Then mi amor I know sure your lips are dawn.

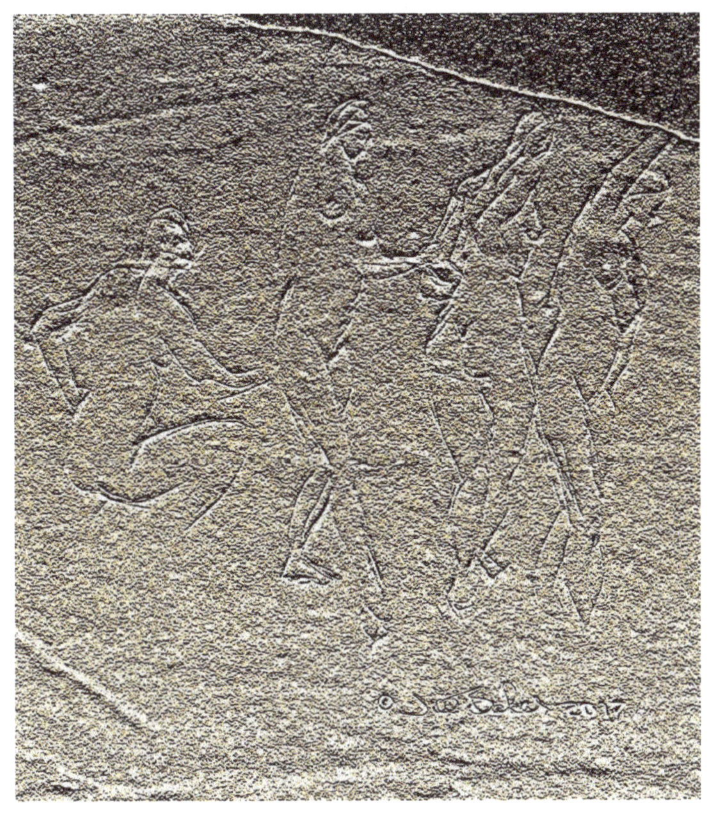

To Hear Your Voice

TODAY IS THE DAY

Today is the day to dance with your soul to hold the
charm of love
between your lips to sing a song of wish of hope and
dream
to spread autumn leaves across fields stubble blond
earth
bound in ways of length and warm clashing thoughts
in stream.

Today is time to hold light between your teeth to
smile a sun
shine ribbon across your face to feel rhythm wind tell
stories of leaves that shake and slither across grass
and oh water clear water in cool deep well.

Today every torn event from pages in ritual passage
rite
storm of favor lifted by arms wrapped in night
embrace
we have set our feet in tightly woven patterns
of sand where washy tides remove every trace.

Today I hold your thoughts bright and wingless
spread
we've come this way before perhaps time and again
now remain to sew silence round our witness web
no stone upturned no shattered limb no singing wren.

WE CANNOT KNOW

We cannot know what morning holds
nor should we having come from night.
The day star spills love over all of us
awakes with her soothing light.

We cannot hear waters flip or turn
our dreams sometimes too tight to let us in.
We must first sit on banks among the fern
listen for the mist to call our name.

The wind whispers what we need to hear.
Leaves precious green wave and sway
this dance of love and light all in one
this place where all deepest secrets stay.

Lovers need not fret nor pine what is lost
merely accept such gift from earth.
Love breeds love surely as hate breeds hate
the weight of which claims our total worth.

AS YOU TURN TO FACE

As you turn to face the morning
know wind awaits moments of your hair
the sun a mirror for your face
rain fingers in dark corners
of clouds give you water peace
earth holds your feet bare
against her skin alive. As you run
know moments of you are
a willingness to life and love
a hope a shadow your shadow
runs with you as your guide
near hidden corners of your mind.
Be not afraid let your laughter rip
open the universe let your holy feminine
halo the whole universe.
Trust yourself
your shadow
let yourself be
bow to you are.

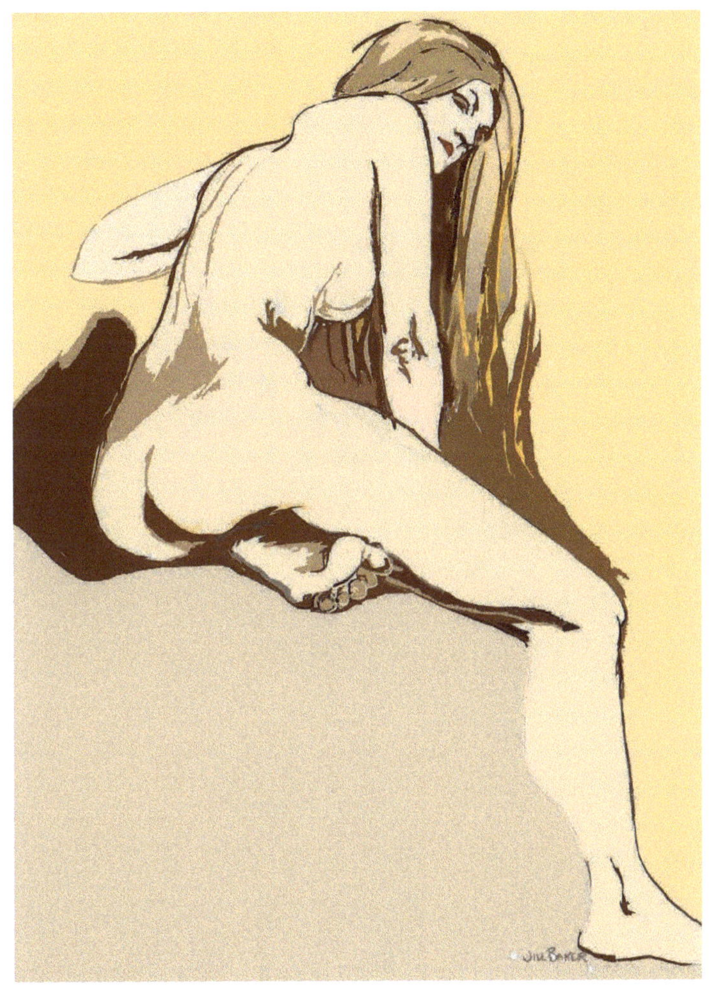

As You Turn to Face

HAIR

Hair he said. Hair she asked. Yes hair.
What kind of hair? Oh everywhere hair.
Cat hair rubbed backwards in dark
tiny star sparks telling time to space.
Waving seaweed hair moved dream
green like worshiping sea hair.
Mane of horses flying wind hair
string of songs across the plains hair.
Eyelash hair talking butterfly talks
whispered thoughts never thought hair.
Hair of the spider geometrically
mocking sun's own light hair
catching prey in her damp lair.
The moon aglow with wisdom hair.
Everywhere hair and even yes even
that hair there. This hair?
Yes. What's so special about this hair?
It is your holy hair
the goddess beauty hair
Sirens sing everywhere her hair.

I CANNOT HOLD

I cannot hold a world's weight
and not first be true.
I cannot bind a sun's light
without a dream of you.

I cannot clutch a wind
tightly to my heart
and still not feel water's rush
or some deeper river's part.

I stand one foot here in light
the other clearly in the dark.
I hear whale's lonely cry
even music of the lark.

I am a child of earth and sun
of wind and rain and such.
I carry always both sad and love
and feel their feather's touch.

Whether you stay or run away
I cannot stop the pull.
Born this way I have no choice
but love you deep and full.

I HAVE STOOD HOURS

I have stood hours listening to turn of wind
felt lonely pull of night rustling limbs
that sway and twirl lifting hands dark
toward moments gaunt and leaf filled.

I have listened to songs rich and dark
hope drenched of rain and stream
where light opens eastern morning
come like foxes purple on the land.

I have heard rivers dance their mood
as though some remembrance stood
mountain high where streams begin
carrying light close to water's skin.

I have heard earth wise and wooly
cover her roots deep and torn
like lovers distant holding steady
in space and time their bodies born.

HOW STUNNING TO HOLD THE MUSE

How stunning to hold the muse close to her face
her hair her everywhere to sense electric
sparks jump gaps wait their turn shadows
under trees swaying sun rise beyond
the dripping moon. What world is flesh and blood
spirit spread across noon? To hold that close moment
real one hand night one hand day wind about
at play blades of grass welcoming thoughts
dark and light the sound of feathers
forever lifting flight.

BROTHER TO NIGHT BUT ALSO SKIN

I am brother to night but also skin to light and wind
where motion twists turns of love held close
earth hearts witness weight wonder send
birds flutter flight inside brings light to rose
red and wet dew tremble now soaked new in dark
wrapped round mercys thrust brilliant and bright
as any song the poet sings melody kindly of lark
wren fresh lifting flesh music to greater height
willing then to know holy glow not quite ours
gods wonderment spread over us through salt and air
what we first thought seconds were really hours
times claim will be never the same I swear

I HAVE BEEN TORN

I have been torn by life's content
rebel yet beyond silence ring
I've told wind where to blow
asked rivers where to sing

I've run with wolves wild and tame
walked with giants where angels fear
have flown on eagle wings
saw earth far below and near

I have been friends with sun and rain
have held to vines of wooden hurt
heard voice new babies sing
known earthworms inside dirt

I've walked a rusty rail or two
I've swam rivers wide
I've known love and hate alike
and breaking of tide

Nothing more can be said
than thoughts torn out of grief
no more than any weeping bride
can give the night relief

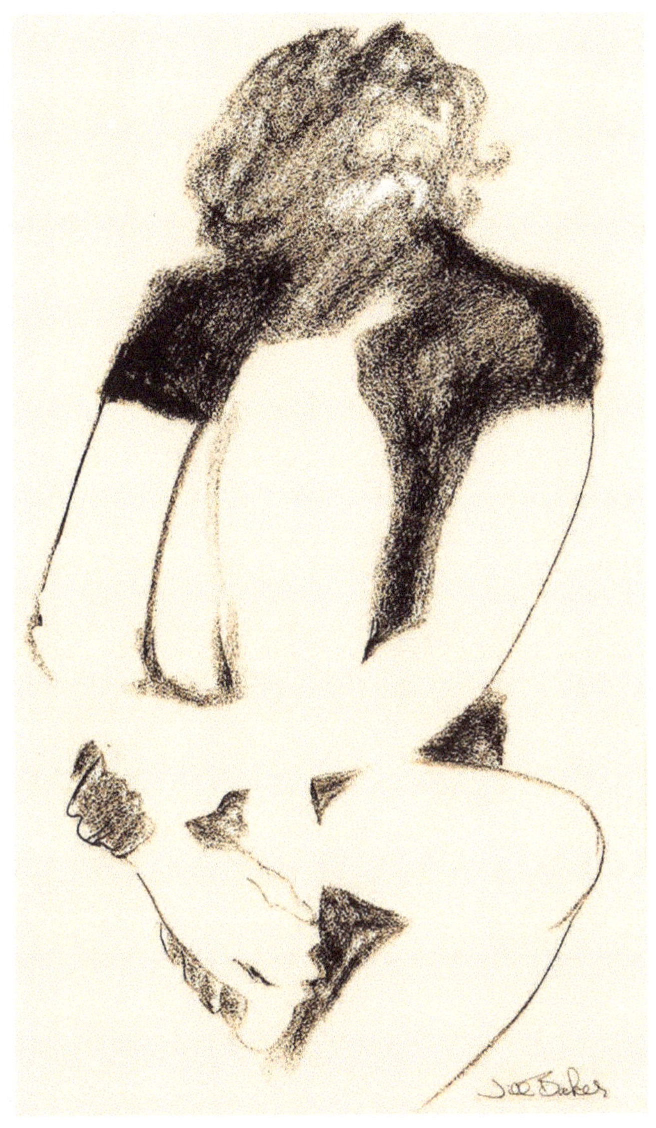

I Have Been Torn

ON THE WINGS OF

On wings of thought I dance rover wise
turn night into things playful and heart
swim with fish near dolphin sounds
spread across water warm and wild I hold
therefore a taste of honey my lips afire
with songs such submerged in depths
only dreamed who can hide seaweeds
green flowing fingers that turn away
as night born of sun who can run will
of wet tie of time haunt of silence
some distance place not yet found not
yet done life little more than quietness
born of rage and whirlpools love claiming
our own circles our labyrinth our run where
tones of light spill across some visual plane
no time left now nothing to complain

PASSING

Death will take you soon my love.
He be near and will guide you where dead go.
Be not afraid my love night is not so clear
Nor that great red road I told you of.

I too now ready for that moment's grace
Impending here beyond the door of spring.
I would not turn the tide even if I could;
You have earned this journey's place.

So I spill love across your slow breathing form.
It sounds so much of wings, wind and rain.
Time now is careless throughout the day.
I watch in grief though will not complain.

I HOLD TO EARTH

I hold to earth though wind pass by
rivers flow toward their dark intent
singing songs a mirror of the sky
their paths a way holy music sent.

I reach for wind in ways I cannot touch
know deep in something moves about
I watch leaves their movement such
I hear their deep and silent shout.

I spread my arms always to catch sun
I hold truth his warmth will bring
I know light and dark are one
day song the night will sing.

I think of rivers now force of dream
have stood by them long and wide
each voice lifts silence greater stream
deep crystal sounds my always guide.

GLANCE

Glance across the room covered with music night
rush of whisper black bird songs and owls who who
your eyes spill light smile yes hello a leaf flutter
silent in trees touch of wind quiet flowers lift
dresses bright as love smile true silver touching air
light spreads fields blond bright gold catching sun
magic gravity line between our dark pool eyes
time cannot contain this moment like roses wrap
knot in wild rush of vine leaves and thorn
brief yet forever cast onto us seas rise and hold
memory close hearts warm while souls wait
patiently where everything condenses explodes
instant rapture caught briefly in trance
dance round and round us in simple glance

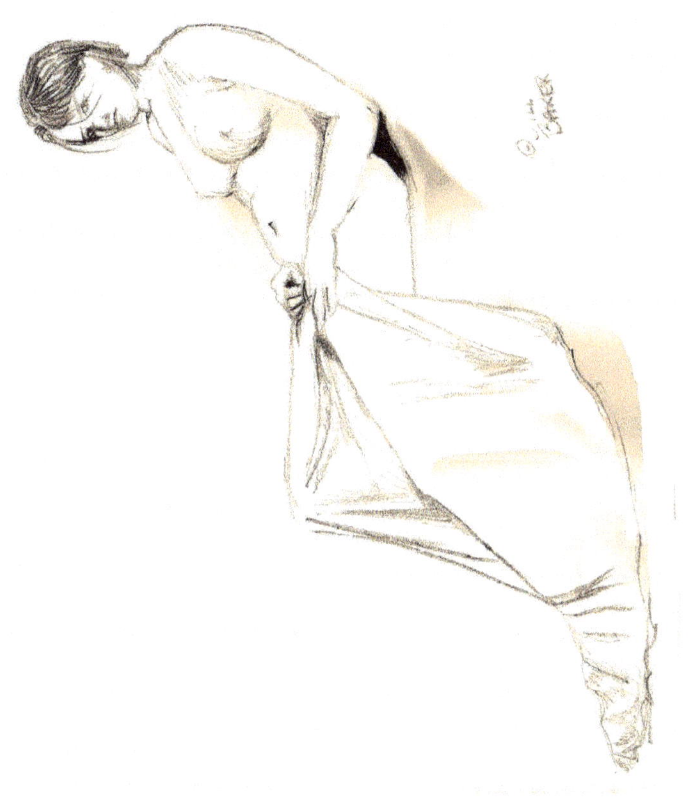

Glance

SMELLS OF SPRING AND LOVE

The morning smells of spring and love
wild birds sing warrior songs
night slips quietly beyond trees
great dark roots hide miniature
shoots little buds spring up pop and turn
and why am I barefoot on grass with dew
wise as wind soft as blue warm rain
at this very moment thinking of you

WHEN YOU DECIDE

We know already where this will go danger
having been abandoned. No matter where
that moment stood glowing red with fire
between love and misery exploding light
never again quite the same now
at best a re-creation of what if.
Such moment comes once
in that special awful everywhere
dream silence unaware
forever beyond our reach.
To time we look; it grants no reason.
We conformably cling to bone thoughts
we dreamers never fail to have.
To wonder what lost what might have been
what never was we now think
through clear brightness of why
how where and when.
Bound to fear of wisdom

we fear we may try again
safely away from electric peril
with paradise lost or never was
we land always on new
continents already familiar.

I COULD CLIMB THE WORLD'S WONDER

I could climb world's wonder rainbows and sky
toward some plane drawn and warped standing still
roads covered with fallen trees grasses waving by
in distant fading dream like quivering hill

against falling light sun lost to night
I could roam dancing thoughts above
what must surely be conceived brilliant sight
of all that's left of rosy fingered love

I could sing darling things against your lips
whisper wet voice things wise in your ears
if you're willing to listen to hearts silent ships
waves splashing against foggy atmospheres

I could hold you close in loves embrace
tame night in one moment greatly blessed
lift your life and dream time and space
sing to that bird that flutters in your chest

AIR

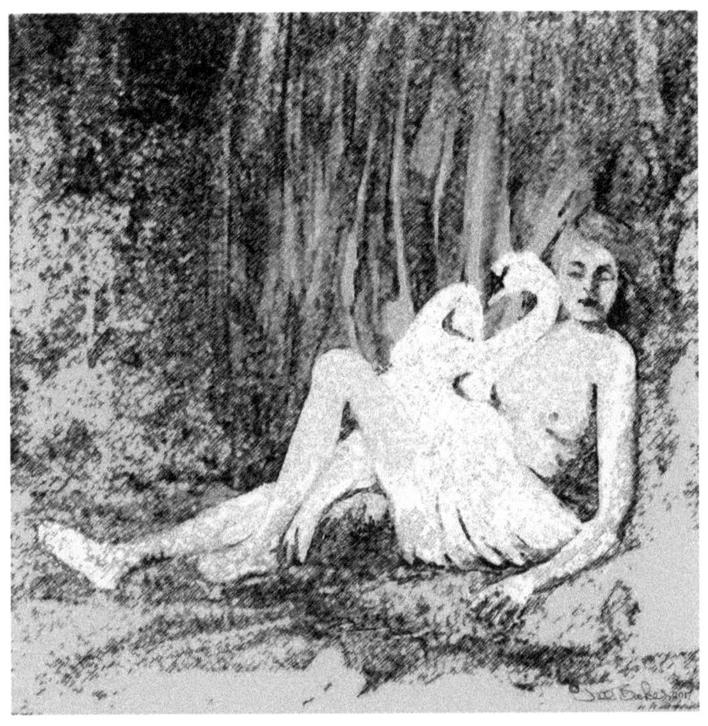

IN YOUR VALLEY

In your valley of beauty
you gift my hand with energy
I linger long at your mystery
sensing dark wakening
life lightning brings.

In valley of hopeless dream
you gift my hand with light.
I walk toward some dark plain
torch held high above my head
see shadows scatter night.

In silent mist that covers us
no sound at all except rain
we move toward unknown wake
to such strange welcoming.

I WILL DISAPPEAR

I will disappear
into your heart
into you
I will
that moment
be you
that moment
you will be me
that moment
will we be.

I HEARD A DOOR CLOSE

I heard a door close today
behind me in the garden of love.
Its sound was like whisper thought
of hands around a trembling dove.

I cannot now look back with dread,
Nor can I look ahead with sorrow.
The sun today will rise in finger clouds.
There will be light or dark again tomorrow.

But oh that sound I've heard before
when I hold hands with the light.
Doors to love open wide for me
then close strangely in night.

ALTHOUGH YOU MAY BE AIR

Although you may be air I hold you just as tightly
as if you were somewhere a great stone warm in my
arms
or some growing tree lifting skyward limbs and
leaves
and if in turn the distant motions sway tell me
standing some distance aside that you are not there
that in the sometime blowing you are no more than
air
I still count it a blessing to feel tug of wind
to see wild spreading and waving of leaves
and oh such blessing just to feel your breeze.

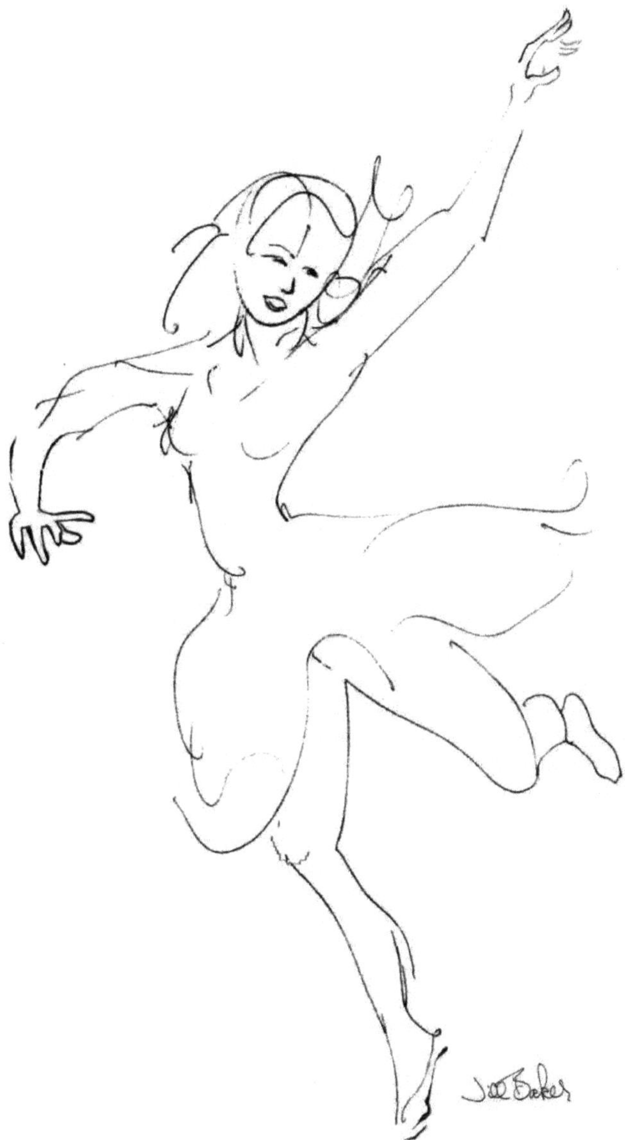

Although You May Be Air

COME DREAM WITH ME

Come dream with me my love
Where clouds wait patiently
Weave their great white puffy
Strands of thoughts and love
High above our destiny.

Come dream with me my love
On nights which suddenly
With grace gift us here
As if some thought magic
Holds our hearts our fear.

Come dream with me my love
While dawn light creeps
Among trembling flowers
Breaks all bonds that free
Dreams in waking hours.

HITCHING A WIND RIDE

I wait here hitching a ride with the wind
time no matter thoughts hang heavy as leaves
ripping rivers ride past where dreams
clean and wildly dance over stones
made glass smooth sound clear whistle
clouds above in argument with the sky.

I've turned this direction and that and stand
guessing now no ride will come or if it does
will pass me by I've counted little motion
in leaves moments of memory
shape of hands rocking the air
I breathe in and out and in again

yet dare not chance pillow of night.
Lovers past ride by in hot rods wave
and scream laid back in convertibles
their laughter shrill as five o'clock blast
of steam when half the factory goes home
and the rest measure their last shift
in apples and cream.

WOMAN WALKING

Today I see beauty walking
talk to air near eve
stop for a moment
in my stare then stand
by cut green where I am.

My arms hold her
briefly in that space.
My eyes forever on her.
Words pass softly
back and forth of love
of things unaware of care.

My eyes follow
her away every step
every turn every low.
She blesses the day
yet will she ever know
if I don't stop here now
to tell her so?

I DO NOT WISH FOR ALL YOUR DREAMS

I do not wish all your dreams come true
there would be too great a pile of them.
I wish only for that one that holds you
that guides your heart in darkness
where firefly light fills you with awe
of the great wonder around all of you.
The dream that comes silently to you
whispers distant call across still waters.
Be ready oh be ready when it comes.
It is there ever so briefly awaiting your grasp
waiting your touch. Take it. Hold it close.
Even if you don't know its name embrace it
even as morning sun embraces your face
even as the wind calls your name in hair
even as spilling waters tell your secrets deep
even as earth holds you closely to her face.
Somewhere out there a spider
writes your initials in her web.

As you walk through fields in season
look for your own geometric wonder.
It is spun in your heart. It is thread night
confined in your own dream web.

A QUESTION THE BUDDHIST REFUSES TO ASK

Is it dangerous
to wash your
panties
and my
shorts
in the same
load?

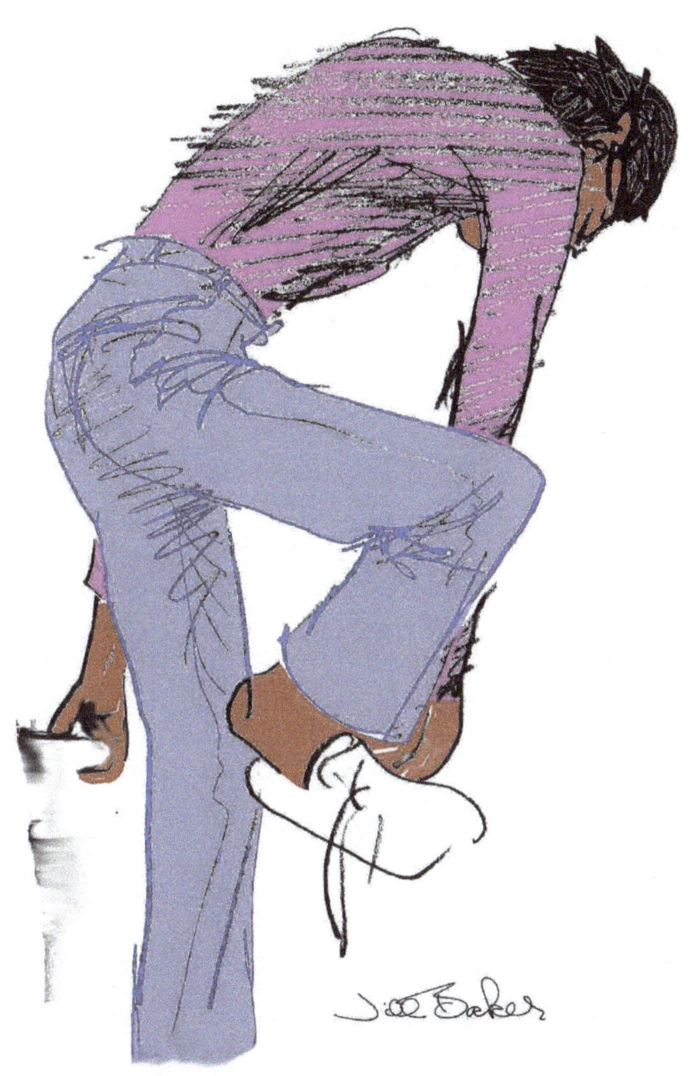

A Question

LOVE IS

Love is a butterfly
with wings that soar
and stain
even
the slightest touch
is capable of bliss
and pain.

IN LIGHT OF WIND

In light of wind in warm of night
deep of space of day and dream
you come to set the record right
stand dawn close lips and might

songs spring up and over us
old guitars now memories seem
I hear whispers near and far plus
frogs jumping rainbows making fuss

love turns lost moments in our hands
It can't be far from silence beam
music pours distant from voice bands
together once where she stands

I hold to this yet trouble throws
our hearts close to heavens gleam
around all wind darkness blows
quite in arms where light grows

your voice clear as hearts content
strings rise up rich and scream
just what all the universe meant
Eve's holy day her apple spent.

I HEARD A WOMAN

I heard a woman call my name just this side of dream
I wake to listen to look for her from where the voice came.
Yet all is silence except that glow that lingers round my face.
I listen look see not nor hear not a glimpse not a trace.

It's not such strange that worries me nor silence now nearby
it is a sound my mind holds still and all the reasons why.
Oh I have lived on voices edge and I have died between.
I remember every voice now gone every face I've seen.

I stand now beside journey's path I wonder at the end.
Cloud people gather pass on by caught by crawling wind.
I a lover of the night hold to that place truths transcend
I am arrow before the flight caught at bow's farthest bend.

MAY WAY OF WIND

May way of wind walk your way
when sun lifts clouds red delight
when water splashes in your dreams
down from rocky mountains dark.

May your journey's walk
challenge you both heart and whim
a trail of briar and flowers be.

May you know or find your way
across rough land or raging sea.

May open eyes clear path you choose
or even one not by you
may you walk with head held high
when storms are passing through.

May you arrive where you want
when you want to be.
May every step that you take
enrich embrace some memory.

And may you find as you go
life so full it bursts with love
for those gone by here before
for those yet standing far above.

They are but one in space and time.
They are both land and sea.
They are at once who you are
who you're yet meant to be.

NOT BY DREAM NOR WHISPER

Not by dream nor whisper relevance
I've come this way in tandem
held wind's embrace and time
world gone blank
ashes bird set to fly
now regions lost and lore.

Held hope not less than love
nor songs mermaids sing
I've walked where eagles soar
sky white and trying
held blanket wish screams
saw dawn slowly dying.

I've reached endless points
of no return now claim
forces high and mighty
I've bent the light
turned the sun
heard awesome crying.

The weight I carry is not my own
nor any earthbound silly
whatever comes does on its own
accepted willy-nilly.
I now trust time more than space
and both more than honey.

LOVE IS WIND

Love is wind in leaves
fire crossing distant plains
water singing over stones in some stream
sun playing with shadows
love everywhere motion and still
love there always yet no time there
hugs kisses embrace
a moment silent that screams heart
dawn loses night and gains light
dusk loses light and gains night
whispered on lips forgotten
love is the perfect yes

MAY YOU HEAR WHISPERS

May you hear whispers of your own soul even as
trees hear wind.
May you know your roots all tiny tentacles that reach
down and out
even as an oak whose roots in distance grows
all together more than twice around the earth.
May your love be greater than your enemies greater
than passing anger
greater than thoughts flying through space
may it swell so much each day that love is even
larger than you.
May you always find hope in unexpected places.
May your dreams walk on water fly wingless above
hover around your aura.
May you listen to voices who call you may you
answer those in need.

May you always always think first of earth whose very heart
gives you passage on your voyage through space.
Love hard hate little. Be at peace with yourself first then with others.
Join no clan whose purpose is to do harm to others.
Be kind to the flowers the stones the grass
the four legged the winged ones the crawlers the swimmers in the sea.
Respect all life and all non life which if you only knew is also counted among the living.
Know happiness and joy where you are not where you might be.
Let the light of your own journey guide you when the trail gets narrow and dark.
Know that light and dark are merely walls
for each other and the side you walk on is entirely up to you.

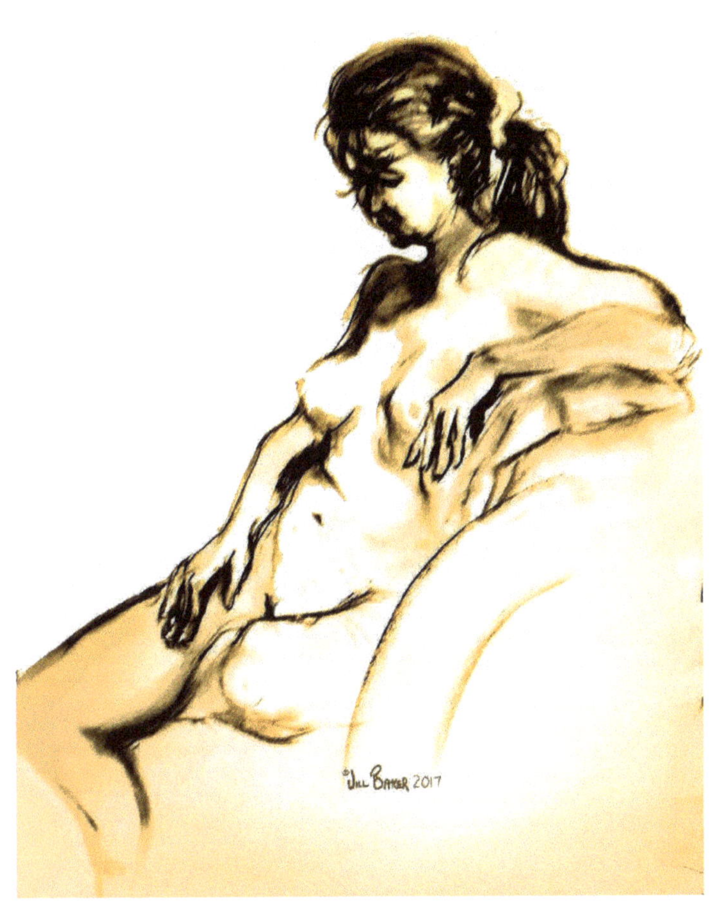

May You Hear Whispers

TRUST THE WIND

Trust the wind she blows a sweetly air.
Hold to earth that nightly turn of light.
Some morning sun awaits tip of grass.
Water from sea finds darkened sky.

Be bold with love as your dreams aware.
Of course stones talk throughout night!
Little rain spots dance where they pass.
Clouded sun will finally tell you why.

Give earth your body to her care.
Release your heart a kite flying high.
Wind now is your only looking glass.
Welcome her as she blows you by.

NOT IN VAIN DOES THE WIND BLOW

Not in vain does wind blow it seeks gentle forces of your face
there to hold motion around your skin then search you bare
as moments make love and thought now in tight embrace
where whispers entangled and wild leave you aware
forces on some higher plain hide here and there.

The wind is not so dumb not to know all of you yet to be
witness higher things than fingers care and hold
slip across your skin light as dream now set free
everything we have held dear and have been told
truth singing beauty to each other as days of old.

The wind willingly finds an altar of your sacred place
claims in dance more than waving universe of hair
all the gods swing happily while heartbeats race
love climbs step by step heavens great stair
yes oh yes screams the wind blowing there.

OH IF THE WORLD WERE ONLY THOUGHT

Oh if the world were only thought
each moment a flower held
glass time filled with sand
attuned to dreams fall
freed from butterfly hand.

Oh if night were only wish
stored fireflies in some jar
their light mere stars of delight
to break the holy darkness
then somehow set it right.

Oh if wind were only hope
come to us those times of need
a happy face among the leaves
turn limbs green and up
magician trick up our sleeves.

Oh if rivers were only songs
ears attuned to mist and wet
earth lifting up her shawl
violins rushing through our hearts
would we hear the singing all?

THE REAL QUESTION

With sense of wisely loss and terrible gain
we stand witness to such height
feel and see that star tiny quiet
twinkly burn everywhere lights remain

Breath back from great release
screams hang still with such delight
memorys moment now interim quiet
once you held Jason's precious fleece

Are you water splash or moving sand
thought wave special wonder of it all
questions form queue in silent crawl
dreamy eyed come to where you stand

The real question to ask is not why
karma rode unsaddled over dream
instead was there an awful fluttering
in silent clouds did you fly did you fly

THERE ARE NIGHTS TO REMEMBER

There are nights to remember days to wonder
thoughts kept secret else the universe tremble
unmistakably hearts flutter hope rattles her bones
wise owls wink and blink and twist their heads
something behind more important than front.

There wings flight weigh dreams
light tears asunder false guess claims night
roses sing red tender yet no small bliss
this moment strikes blessed thunder
dark clouds embrace December.

There is way with snow dark landscapes covered
white and bleak pure concealed ways of dark
all blemishes of love hide beauty torn wake
sound scorns light burn of thought
transcend souls grinding hearts intent.

Welcome birds fly in circles
dark Rorschach sky claims deepest
dreams we dare moments screams
laughter our willingness moans delight
darkness opens wide accepts light.

WHEN YOU FEEL WIND IN YOUR HAIR

When you feel wind in your hair I am there.
When white snow falls around each flake
thoughts hold you the crystal light.
When you hear mother speak it is my voice also.
When sun seeks out your bodys ways
it is also my light that moves and sways
thoughts always around you inside you.
What you feel is not some distant drum
bringing wind spirits long and far away.
I am dark that wraps your holy form
I am light that brings you warm.

WIND MOVES SILENTLY

wind moves silently across the green
lifting dresses of queen Anne's lace
frogs hide in the grass voyeurs croaking
guttural sounds at end of bubble lips
river tumbles across nose of land
finds welcome grass bent its way
turn of light falls willingly west
hides sounds in dark yet to come
along bank tiny five toed prints
escape south and south west hands
imprint in mud saying drink
or escape or both toward dawn
night is happy fellow here winking
stars above know light will come
dance with him song of motion
heart beat drum along horizon edge

FORGIVE ME

Forgive me if I dream your dark mystery
wrapped around me in love's delight
whisper winds tell the leaves
all the birds will soon be to flight.

Forgive me if I reach for you
dream and dream you close in night
feel your beauty weighted with love
surround my all reach new height.

Forgive me if I love you so
where only dreams can set it right
and if I hold you close this way
feel all your power of love's might.

Forgive me if choice and not
are warriors of a single fight
a battle we both know by now
more than either dark or light.

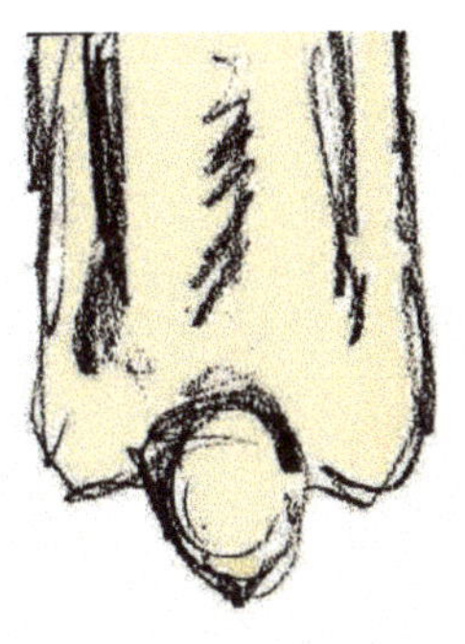

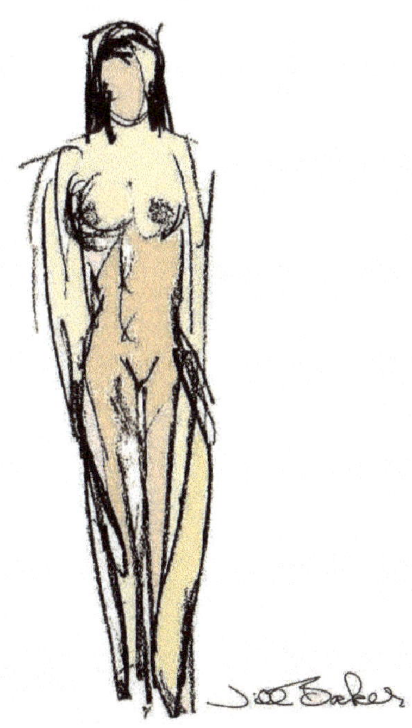

Forgive Me

ON PROMISE

The flow of lifeblood energy much depends
on promise hope and dream spread
like light coming or rays falling west.

Take away dream and waking hour
attempt at sleep where none will come.

Take away hope water streams dry quickly
move lower till trapped minnows jump and jump
to higher light hopeless of course that upward flight
that thrusts them rudely back to earth.

Take away promise darkness comes raggedly
awaits nothing where freely
night rolls into another layer on layer
old onion of blackness everywhere.

PICTURE

Although I cannot physically see you through
walls through trees through the splendid air
I hold that somewhere in my blind vision
you must stand over there somewhere.

You must do all those things others do
eat and dress and undress and sleep
I picture you resting on your chair
thinking promises you have to keep.

Maybe you too watch pictures not quite there
but float to you on screen invisible across air
perhaps your run fingers through your hair
just for a moment realize I am aware.

At last I picture when you rise up prepare
falling waters for the body's nightly dance
you softly slide soap over your skin's wonder.
It's then I dream or think I see I swear.

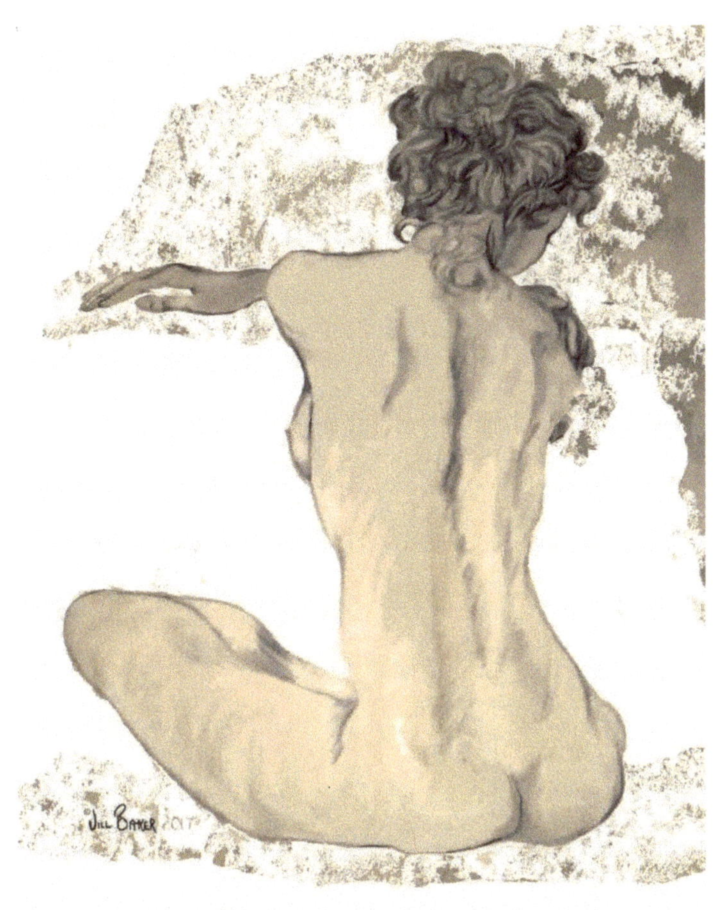

Picture

I CANNOT CLAIM THE WIND

Though I am brother I cannot claim the wind.
Rain finds me tender wets my face with smile.
I know then his wetness kin. I live and love
where earth eats sun and things greener
than I turn hearts to wondering.
Oh if I could only twist silence back to rain
surround my heart with love's highest beat
I could know the grasshopper's final rest.
The night's no longer young still I am blessed
the soul dangles on a chain in space
tender moment I in distress turn to face
what rising sun a sky torn wrapped in lace.
No regrets for streaming cloud not yet met
held in place drums waiting sounds relief
this be merely dark conquest of night
no time nor inclination for such belief.
I am here to challenge escape of light.

I WALK WHERE WINDS HOLD LIMB

I walk where wind holds limb dark fingers touch her
face.
I wonder as sun speaks light while soils rest in place
where waters rumble tumble their dreams dancing
dash stones and rooted trees I am breeze

not whisper voice I hear from far away.
Night slips to sleep and day dark clouds weep
terribly across the sky. I cannot wonder where to
burn
to wave and wave goodbye. Still I turn to this

moments sure as love real as nights conquest.
I lover tumble with streams hold light where I can.
Perhaps I am butterfly flittering above land
nectar exploding honey bees their wings complaint.

I am no hero I am no saint. I ride ocean waves
crash surf in time. I eat seaweed stuff
to be seas great mystery to be hearts content.
I no more than wind or loves brief consent.

FIRE

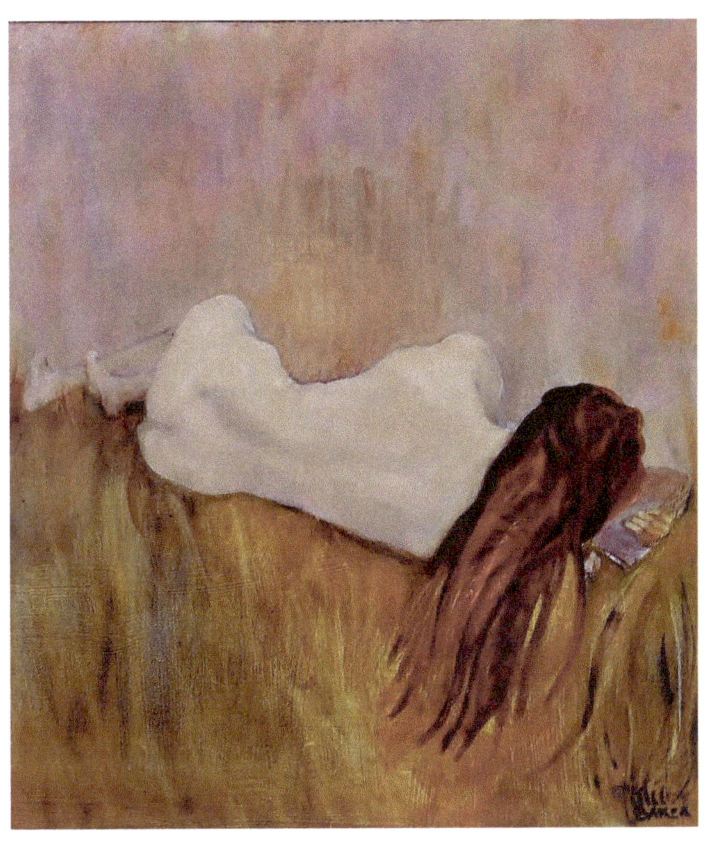

A TASTE OF FIRE

You gift me with fire tongues touching lips ablaze
in that moment I dream your dark valley
spread wide for me, You welcome me into your siren
way wrap music boldly around my dripping love
guide me wildly deeply into your scream.

Free now from mast I hear your song
burning and licking my flame
teasing my flutter heart like a bird.
My mind dances your swing and sway
precious darkness held this way.

SO THE DAY BEGINS

So day begins with birds singing in light
a soft wind barely waking leaves
night crawlers having stayed a night of love
craw safely back into their holes alone.
In this moment of now Zen sun rises on faith
where such wait welcomes weightlessness
of the floating dance I am we are.
I have heard the same story this song before.
I have also told it more yet each time new.
I stand now listen to the weep
feel sorrow for fading night loss of dark.
I at one linger below upon between
happy swells on horizon's edge

BLINK OF LOVE

I come from corners of time waiting my turn
my toss my burn. You there by the open wind
swirl around my thoughts like leaping birds
wait my call held like torches above your head.

I have no complaint with shadow nor shade
nor light so focused there is willing burn.
I simply come this way softly walking
abiding by nature's wonder force of love.

And if I hold you wise and willing nights
where fireflies on and off turn their lights
will you also blink and blink in search of love
moving across moments dark delights?

LIGHT MOMENT

In morning fog my thoughts stretch across
a gray curtain cloud down from trees
night still a whimper of katydid sounds
fireflies talk light and blink
love moments everywhere.

The grass damp where angel tears
cover green where spider tents color of clouds
wrap geometric wonders on stems and stones
little droplet eyes wait the hidden sun
to dance across diamond bones.

Holding this moment a burden lovers share
stardust streaks across the sky
lines glow a moment brilliant
then silently black back to memory
where once gold light slid.

Morning comes objects crawl
from shadows dark and fine
birds sing notes awake near and far
just before that moment light too much
you and I another meteor are.

SISTER TO THE MOON (for Jill)

In the middle of the moon of changing seasons,
the goddess rises full behind your eyes. I hold
you close feel your song against my chest
our hearts dueling drums matching beats.

Perhaps a first this is the way goddess light covers
you reflects you while rainbow leaves tremble
their colors dancing free around your feet.

I watch her light come into your light
and your eyes bring light back on me.
I hold a goddess bathed in goddess light
two enchanted sisters promising night.

YOU WHO INSIDE A CANDLE BURNS

Easier for us my love to be nude than naked words.
Words protest their bare skin and candles burn, yes
candles burn. We can walk quietly touching touch
throw light back among our reaches. But firemen
in their blood red trucks hunt out those untamed
fires that consume us much so near the heart. Those
naked words evacuated dance over us they too
spill light as candles bright they too contain the burn
while you and I walk skin to skin I a candle in
your dark glow now with all of your naked light.

SO HOW DOES THIS HAPPEN

We didn't talk beforehand to say we'd each do that or
this
yet here we stand face to face this moment now and
you
point out likenesses--hope and desire
as if some greater plan were in place. A major
universal
accident or swift thin fingers of synchronicity?

A greater match I suggest already exists
holds us closer to spirit and bone binds
us tighter than what we witness here in outer dress.

Of all things normal or ab permit me this guess
something greater comes our way
a reckoning beyond full reach
the nature and being of who we are
who we were who we will forever be.

We join flesh to bone spirit to flesh
open a place neither of us has ever been.

We wait here to welcome holy
wonder dark sacred bliss.

Careless night now wakes us
moment electric to this.

WAKING TO LOVE

I wake this morning to love
of grass and leaves of August
held green and a gray sky
gifting drink to thirsty below
and the Persieds having done
their dance--moments of gold
across dark lines aplenty
to write Ogham illusions.

It is this secret code now lost
I write my own destiny in time
will hearts out of the past
watch thoughts explode
star streaks loose from cages

and I stand burned by coming sun
awake to wind encouraged
by dust devils along the road
baby tornados timing their lift
with my own frail swirl
of vortex dreams and dust.

ALWAYS BE READY WHEN MORNING COMES

Always be ready when morning comes
with its bright warm sun horizon red.
Know that moment when birds begin to sing
shadows huddle together for last goodbyes.
Walk in the morning wind
let your face feel coming delight
the day which awaits you.
Walk the trail earth has given you
trail that leads you along in light and dark
finally to the water's edge.
Where wind sun water and earth meet
at that very spot set down your feet.
Feel your body's acceptance of where you are
who you are and realize you are part of
yourself the elements of the universe
that surround you that you are now immersed in.
Now sing your own song
the one only you can sing truthfully.

BEAUTY WALKS

Beauty walks in patterns made thoughts by wind
that holds light terribly toward some kind
of reason beyond one's guess. We cannot touch
this fire except its total flame much
the way a notion expresses dream
we have been just such a stream
filled with more than siren song
gift where light and dark together belong.

DO NOT WASTE THE LIGHT

Do not waste light moments come near and far
corners of the universe hold warm and tight
linger on edges, traces left by some star
fingers running across the wrap of night.

Morning whispers held here now fall
flowers once hidden or lost now found
embedded in your nest your gleam of all
where you awaken life holy sound.

Behold angel dark mystery sings whale songs
air trembling silent no more now scream.
Your heart's dance swirls round and belongs
to one great empty now full with dream.

THE WATER'S FIRE

Only a moment's breath I hold you close
as if dream wakes here sleeping water
silence splashes beyond the stream
calling Leda's daughter.

I touch a voice that lingers now
shapes beyond the fireflies glow
a nightly thought ripple free
moonlight dancing color of snow.

I clutch the moment fist tight and long
and wonder where light has gone
yet praise that dark rich and sweet
held once beyond moment's bone.

I cannot tell you what you know
that's yours alone to contemplate
I have danced the water's fire
you have felt the water's weight.

IF THE WORLD WERE RED

If the world were red would we sing of love or sorrow
If birds flew north in winter's glow would they come back tomorrow
If life shared with us all her secrets dark and deep
would we with laughter sing or hide where shadows weep
If we had hearts made of gold would we share or hoard
If all nights gathered in one pile could we the dark afford
If you and I stood face to face and spoke with eyes aglow
would all the world dream silently everything we know

IF TIME AND SPACE SUDDENLY

oh if time and space fly suddenly away
no more sounds from wing spread thought
can I still hold dream awake if tilted dark
over where wide open turns to naught

can I still hold to eyes wide awake
feel chill of wonder dream and wept
hear wind among the danger leaves
their tiny torsos blindly swept

over wild winter lawns widened snake
do I hold my grip of things dream inspired
night a willing wonder consent lake
beyond cross-like shadows heavy wired

can I not know time no space can grant
that willing gift there again and back
when worlds and lights a westward slant
over roads born red on other track

LIGHT SLIPS IN

Light slips through edge of curtain
Willing silence enchants the mind
like some great red dot torments a cat.
Wind holds no favor but hides
in small green tree branches
glove fingers cover winter dark stems.
In clouds a hint of rain gathers
great foam cups with circling
dark edges held in dawn's breath.
Earth wakes her troop
from grass millions and millions
tiny feet dance walk to honor day.
Sun of morning wakes of wind
burden of clouds
wet love earth again again.

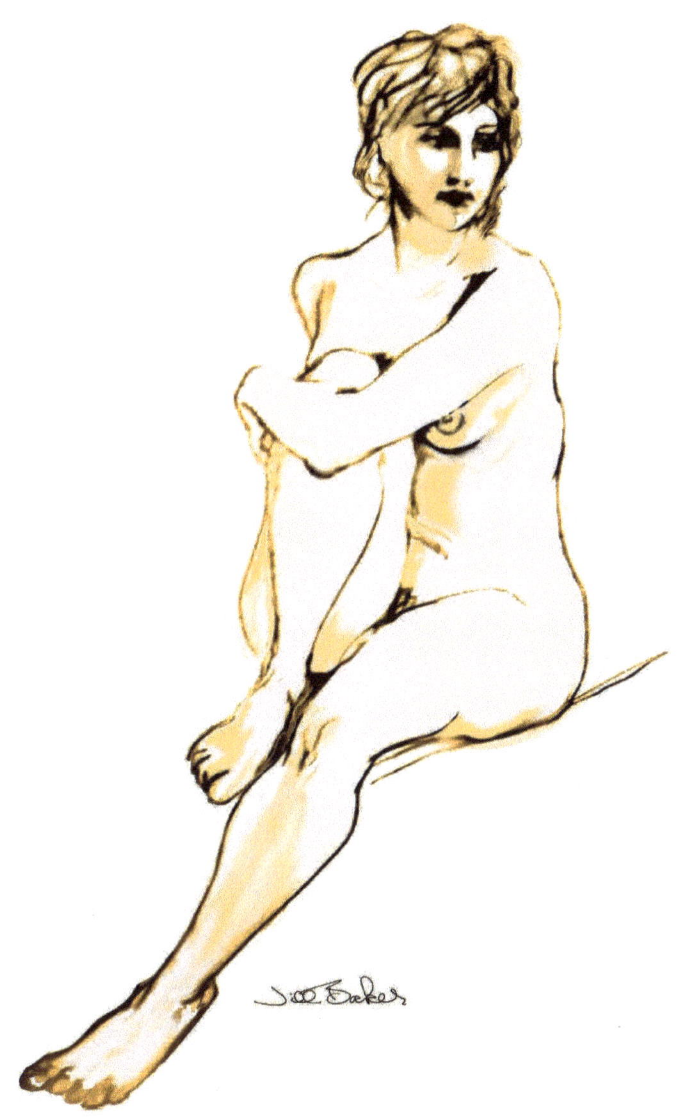

Light Slips In

EVEN NOW

Even now

I hold you against me

our bodies trembling

everywhere

I reach

you are

everywhere

you are

I kiss.

IF WE BURN AND GLOW

If we burn and glow with light of sun and if
we hold stars tight within our chest
if we hear the birds deep in song
while morning rushesin from the west
if we hear sounds of our own hearts
drums awakened deep across the waters
if we touch that moment gripped in grief
where mirror tears be everything that matters
if all warped time come and gone rushes by
if we live each moment as consent
will we walk the silent earth alone or not
will we drink night's dark intent

HOPE YOUR MORNING

Hope your morning if filled with sun
dreams longings to be filled
light around you as guide
night to keep your secrets silent
water to wrap you in thoughts
earth to sense your bare feet

I HAVE BURNED IN SUN'S GLANCE

I have burned in sun's nightmare glance
all the world held its glimmer face
knees trembled like blades of grass
scorpions chased their slithered place.

I have known voice of rain say things never heard
open skies prairie wide and dark concealed
little balls ice people dance a million toes
tiptoe and bounce across plains revealed.

I have watched willow wind push tumble weed
have stood in awe of dust and light
while old barbed fences held new loves
caught at last from tortuous flight.

I have walked across an open earth
content to know I'm just passing through
everywhere I've been every moment
found a dying world born anew.

OUR DANCE OF POETRY

Night wakes bee wings love snakes craw
silently over stone in moonlight a million eyes
stare on stars above dancing light poems of night
we swim in thoughts blank and wonderful
sway our hips against some distant melody
rub flesh against bones not yet born

Out of wisdom comes little dream eagles
spread wide to welcome dawn and other such
flowers along a creek bend their singing heads
toward waters way and you and I in dance
winds and limbs and roots deep at play
earth casts a face of dawn from all light of seas

Our dance is dance of poetry love sown
somewhere a universe unbroken yet undone
claims of lust where destiny hand moves quill
dark lines steel air birds write ribbons in the sky
messages in tiny snow suits sit quietly still
wait our moments incandescent reply

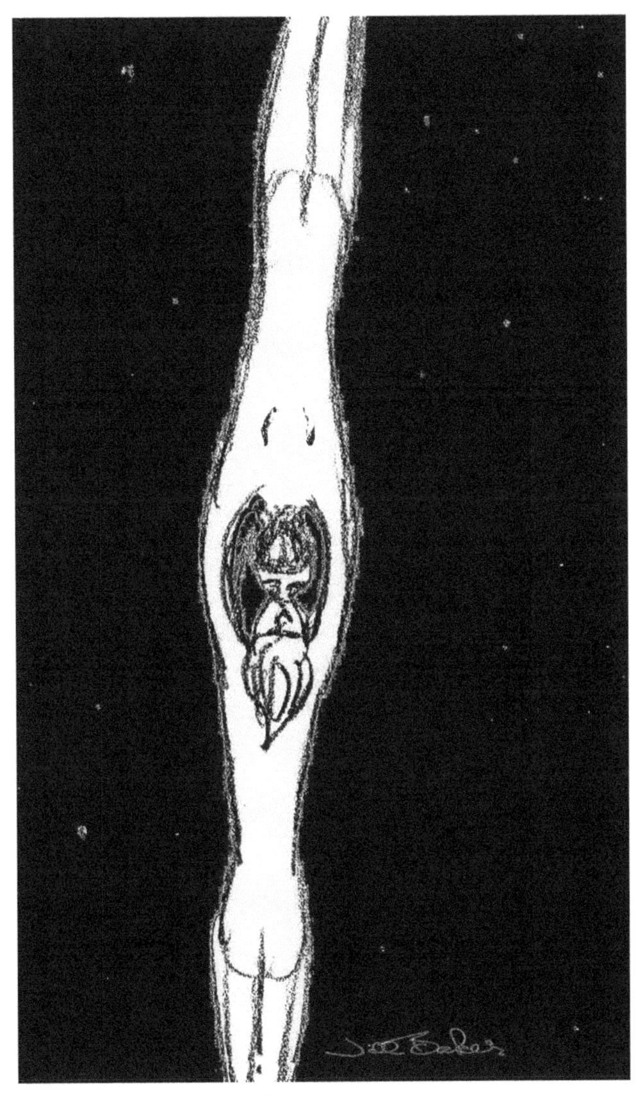

Our Dance

MAY YOUR MORNING

May your morning be filled with love
so great it spills everywhere bright as sun.
May dreams surround you splashing like springtime
streams.
May winds bring you hope abundant.
May the earth hold you close embrace you.
May your heart beat love dreams hope embrace
your own drum sound in this place.

IF ROSES BURNED THEIR TALK IN TIME

If roses burned their talk in time
and held the world at bay
would you move odors waves
have something new to say

If all the wind found your face
and toyed with your hair
would you without moments rest
seek out the foxes lair

If time were a moment spent
and lost all others or gone by
would you sing of torn hearts
or mourn white clouds flowing by

If somewhere alone and lost
you heard a voice warm and wet
would you move toward or away from it
and would you still be there yet

If all the night claimed your thoughts
if all the day came straight your way
would you run somewhere to hide
or seek a dying sun's final ray

I WATCH RISING SUN

I watch rising sun awesome glow
come waiting leaves night's content
my eyes attuned now light anew
darkness farewell just now spent.

I stand hours here dark and light
thoughts past border still in view
all life hangs bright in her web
spider shakes the strings anew.

Shimmer hope eight leg wealth
dance final dance full of time
all move dew soaked as stealth
turn dreams and wish sublime.

You too must hear snow's offence
raging stream held sure afoot
wind messenger now receives
faces drawn dark as soot.

I HOLD TRUE THOUGHTS

I hold true thoughts that willy-nilly race my mind
leave smiles and giggles across life's terrain
I believe in waterfalls and fingers a Zen kind
tested heartbeat worship of the brain
wash beat times open gate and all the wild
turned loose freely fleeing a darkened plane
great wild cloud distance laughter of child
bells silver breaking driving marigolds insane
I have held wings of bees flew their flight honey
sought flowers where nectar flows flame in gain
of sunlight wind dancing bright and runny
time taking measure of life's frail chain
tight around our necks binding us in vain.
screams akin to some captured bunny
runaway horse clinging tight its mane

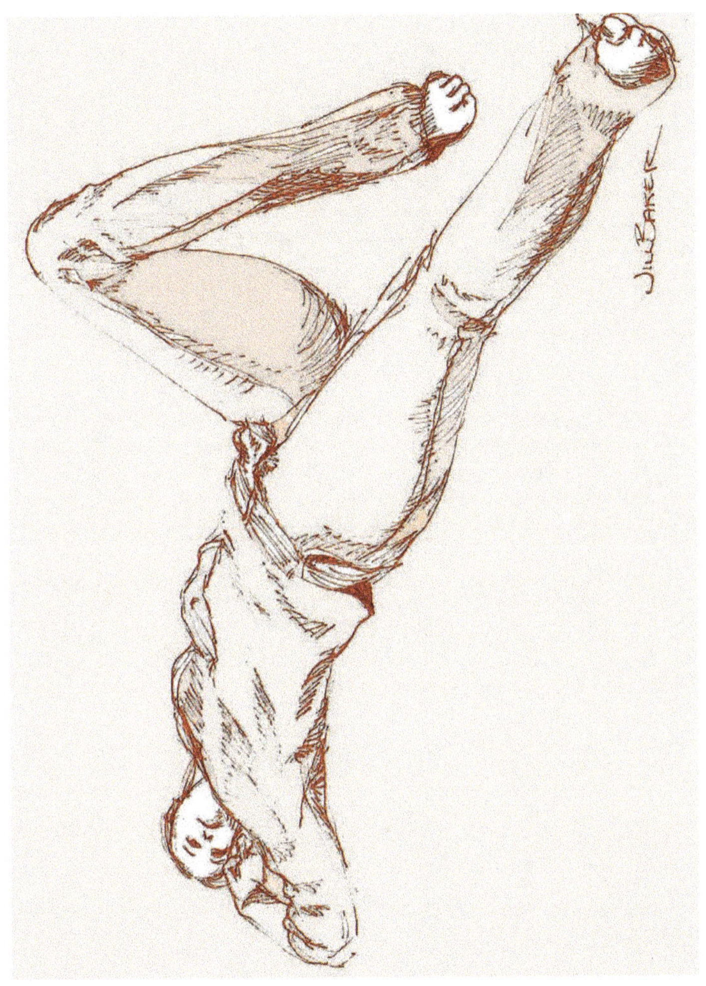
JILL BAKER

LIFE DIPS INTO TINY TOUCHES OF LOVE

Life dips into tiny touches of love
held to fingers like honey dripping
sound falling on waters and wrinkled circles
spreading far and wide deep and silent

We turn each moment holding it to light
wondering watching waiting willing
mirror ourselves in flashing glint
the weight is more than hearts in flight

Time takes us there and brings us back
waves of wonderment splashes wild
night holds no special purpose except
perhaps lovers delight

I CANNOT NAME SILENCE

I cannot name silence held in forks of night
I cannot bare loves honor mirror to the light
all the stage a world all the bird a flight
I hold you deep in my thought but cannot set it right

the weight of song moves quickly silent as a stream
never would I bind the wind in spite what may seem
I just as well would dark the sun take away her beam
or leave the world in loneliness you must know what
I mean

I have such little wisdom to hide among the breeze
I listen to the wildest storms twisting at the trees
I hear a coyote waling then drop down to my knees
for I have sung with the birds flown with the bees

it is now nights turn to burn the dark away
time for clouds to speak windows closing on the day
if you by chance hear of curtains holding hope at bay
listen very carefully know what their shadows say

IF MIDNIGHT EYES

If midnight eyes of hope and fear stare into love's
bright dream
if flashing light torments the dark where banks
contain the stream
if sounds of scream wake the stars that pepper spray
the sky
if sun's welcome rays fall down where ocean waves
goodbye
if in the wind your hear your name spoken again and
then
if all the trees bow down to you where your thoughts
have been
if in your heart you feel that flame warm your holy
dark
if on the sand you draw your name just to make your
mark

if all your world's a sailing ship where you walk the
plank
if life swirls round and round your head and holds
you wise and blank,
fear not that desperate turn and twist the swirling of
the clouds
lightning speaks to you here now through passion of
the gods.

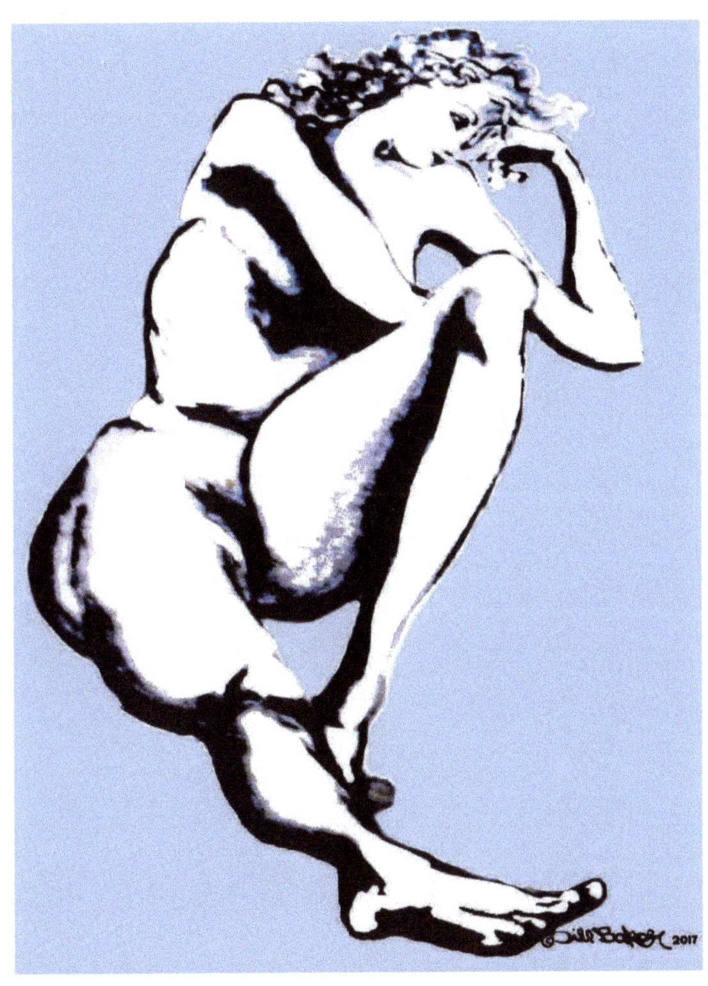

If Midnight Eyes

WHEN YOU

When you swim the sea I am the water that covers you
surrounds your form from tip of toe to hair your lips
your fingertips I splash your knees cover your feet

When you walk the beach I am the wind that follows
claiming moments of your hair your face your eyes
your cheeks getting close to hold you share the sand

When you lie in thought I am the sun that slips down on you
warms your skin braces your thoughts with light terrible
shadows trembling seek everywhere your holy dark

When you are covered with laughter and screams of delight
I am earth gentle where you walk where you hear whispers
near eve's apple I am terra firma entering your divine night

WATER

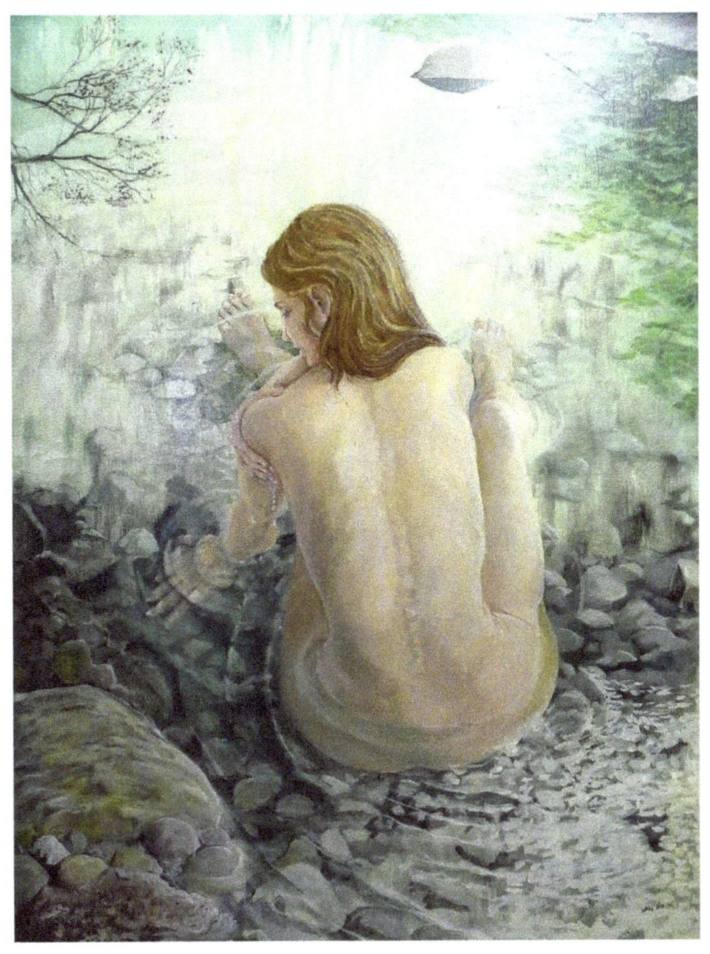

EVEN IF WE CANNOT DREAM

Even if we cannot dream I will never there
unless yes is softly said among the milkweed
like wind breath over dried thistle and only
then if I hear the wild geese honking yes
times deep in Canada now lost on the water's skin
Molly Bloom must also walk the mirror sky
little peeps of sun must yes blink down
little poison leaves yes every which way we turn
welcome us yes where we tip toe between green
blades
our longing thoughts waft where we walk yes
that unbroken dam holds water back
the size of our desires yes least we drown
we move silently there now yes
kisses dance yes over years unaware
we tremble together our lips dare yes
what the rest of us cannot embrace
a thousand white eyes dancing yes
Turk's caps Queen Anne's Lace yes.

WHEN A WOMAN SAYS YES

When a woman says yes stars tremble
and the universe leans toward love
thunder beings wake songs across the land
sky people swim and swirl claim new spaces
not yet found in the great way up there blue
sparrows dart and dance grass bends down
carefully weighing passion tipped in red
burn against the inky way a worship of sorts
below the wind away from curling leaves

When a woman says yes night folds her blanket
rises to tip the rosy fingered dawn
blurred lips speak melodies never before heard
little fingers inquire of dreams on edges of thought
the milky way runs through space carrying its own
sight
in the deep gray distant fog ship horns sound
the tune walks across sacred water
voices held tightly escape disguised as love moans
now released each having waited their turn

When a woman says yes the radiance of day
is no match for her nor her single gift
spread and welcoming sun and flight
nowhere in the cosmos are songs more powerful
no rainbows more brilliant nor any as bright
roses droop pay homage to memory indelible
no match either is her greeted change of day
that moment held mysteriously inside wild delight
her holy dark far more brilliant than any light.

FOR J

You have now shared my bed
with neither bone nor flesh
nor tongues wrapped.

Still our spirits smoke soaked
whisper words of sage
gods now clean with love
not unhappy with our quest
naked ladies rising
roses waiting bud and bloom
the morning blessed.

You have slept where I have slept
held the blanket to your breast
dreamed the same fields
where I have dreamed
felt the coverlet warm
of thoughts and light
sprinkled on dark trails
we've wandered here and there
and everywhere.

You have touched the night
where I have tossed
touched where I have been
turned where I have done
have held your warmth
against my warmth
our lips a waterfalls
lost in swirling mist
our arms wrapped to hold
the body's dance
this gift this trance.

Pounding hearts
drip songs from the corners
of everywhere.
J. Alfred's question
now this oath we share
do we dare do we dare.

GIFT

I've thought of this and maybe question sanity
I who in a moment give all I am to one
whose wisdom of dreams and rain carry
questions fading like mountains release their fog
or leaves lift heavenward in brightness
fingers green as all the love gift life
a wave and dance the same
at once songs that all the singers sing.
What I bring and what you bring make one
not one the two we stand in the same sun
same rain same wind same dream same love.
So if we go this way the question must lie
in corners held by our own bright spiders.
We've come this far attuned to beat and breath
our eyes held in tight commitment.
Such gift cannot be weighed of time and space
we surely realize now beyond all guess.
Of all the things we know it must be this.

IF YOU WELCOME SUCH AS RAIN

How can you hold the warm and damp so close
yet never flinch in darkness webbed this way?
We struggle at the tightness of dawn the wing
weaves star patterns of our dreams. So think
this not some gentle lifting some hopeless gift
that tangles us beyond the wet of warm.
We are delighted by bite of love
welcome this rain that holds the waves
against our lips to taste the salty burn.
Stranded under angel tears their falling
great slowly wraps our gift each to each
where rain walks our faces haunts the sea
of immensity we know neither sky
nor land. Perhaps we can only be what
we be never know gifts of night
never realize the true being of the sea
so great a distance now from our flight.

Lee Pennington

IN DREAMS

In dreams
you swim nude
through clear water
then come ashore
face the rising sun
little jewel
droplets race
down your skin
wet the sand
where you stand.

My thoughts soak
your feminine form
you become
morning sun
in gold water
repeating your name
your feet pressing
the earth
and I
this moment
wishing
I were wind.

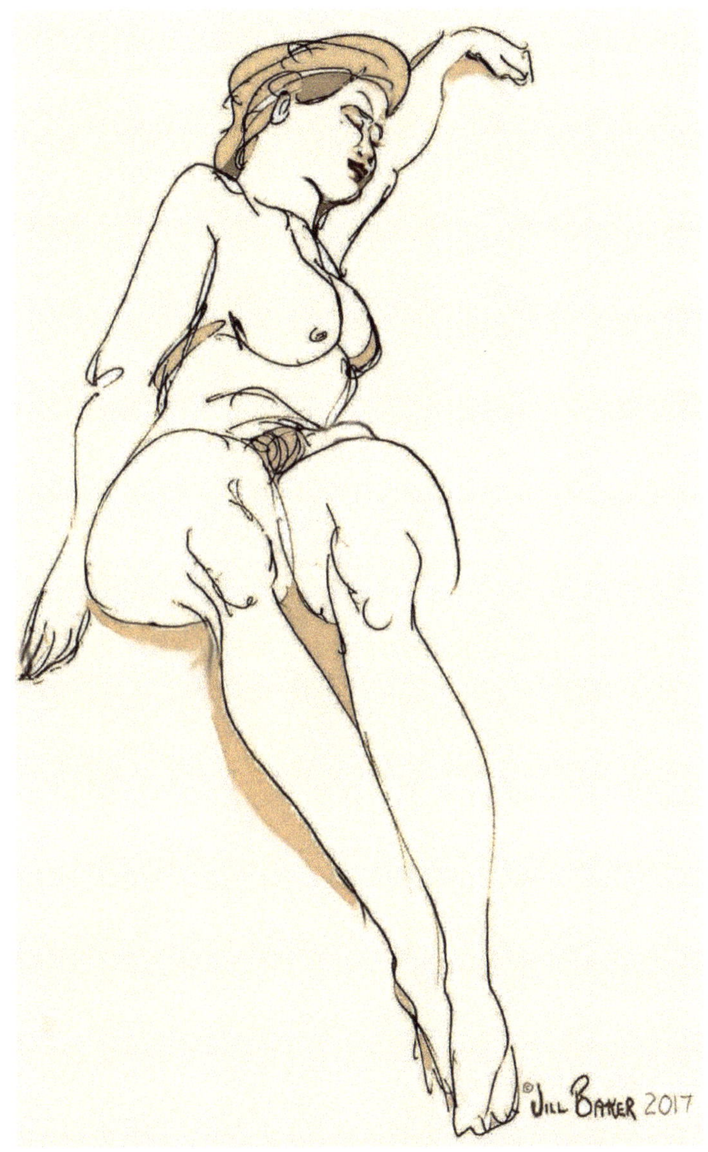

In Dreams

SOUND OF SPLASH

Do I dare hold your image in my stare
you goddess of spring? A waterfalls
surrounds your feminine form and I
jealous of that wetness that holds you there
while my thoughts wrap you unaware.

Do I dare swim this swirl of waves
with love arms swung wide song of wet
where water jumps from stone to beam
inside some salmon's call of dream
to climb again this wall this stream.

Do I dare welcome this sound of splash
this wake of turn tumble spill and swish
blending hair and body white
seaweed woman stained with light
moon glow now walking night.

MAY YOU HOLD THIS MOMENT

May you hold this moment
a grasp of universe
precious where over grass green
thoughts horses romp away
to where you stand in awe
of the river.

May this moment
bless you your world
lift your heartbeat on bird wings
wind flutter toward the holy dark
where all love hides
waiting her turn.

May horses and birds
announce your journey
the blood jungle thunder
a swirl of hearts
a perfect storm
of hope and moment.

May night's hand rest
softly on your thigh
glide slowly upward
toward forever hair
with waves of welcome
that dance you all over
everywhere.

WALKING WITH LOVE BY THE SEA

In gifts of time no star trails trace blended light
across sky nor wind speak leaves against
open space. Yet here we walk by this sea
our prints together sand defined
like memory waves and pipers darting by
we count the bubbles in sifting foam
taste salt captured in spray dreams
a clatter of clouds grants dawn delight
while walking here we barely escape night.
First we sit our feet in front of us our arms
locked each to each in moment wonder
who is who or this vision far beyond our reach.
First dressed then nude (dreams are easy this way)
we let water calm our every thought
bodies and water one water too much us
to know how deep or wide oceans be.
We embrace dream to dream thought to space
water wet to wet enough love. You welcome

me deeper than anywhere I have dreamed or been.
Waves not quite our own not quite the sea
wash round and through our gifted flesh
bodies entangle each until we're no longer us
but something greater than staring eyes see.

YOU WONDER WHY

Just because you connect to them
I love finding words to wrap you in.
They are gift of the muse
who sometimes must be you.
It's brightness
of feminine energy
creative wonder
comes from it all.
Only waters know.
Only wind tells it so.

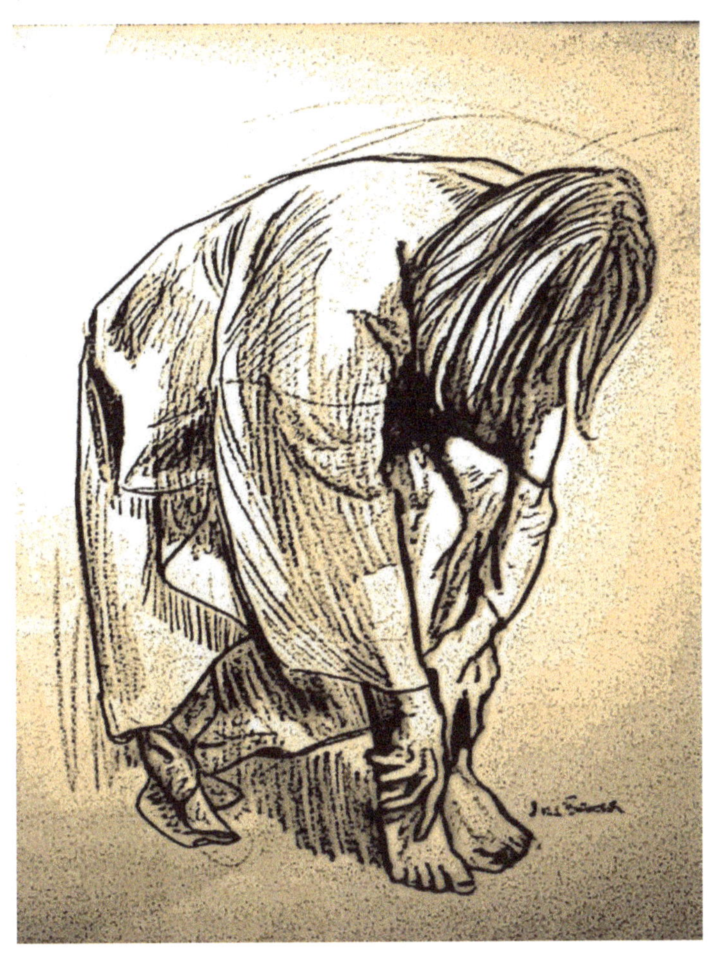

You Wonder Why

A REVIEW OF SORTS

Such a moment carries great voice of whales
all sea's energy in that confine crystal water
gushing sound life bursts around flesh of darkness.

By choice I hold you tight as dream and walk beyond
waking
narrow trail lifted in grace above limbs
all songs birds have hid come from throats freely.

It is day but dark is precious as fire of tongues
speak truth around your being around your thoughts
springs deeply from your wells of light and love.

Oh maiden I hear your song of wind and water
you sing over stones alive with sweet flesh and hair
and I poor Odysseus ears unwaxed listen there.

EVERY DAY BLESSED

The earth beneath a song of walk
autumn leaf is crunch and talk.
Green violins blades of grass
lift their music where we pass.

Wind comes round to touch our face
waving wonder gives voice to place.
Music of these darkly limbs
chance to sing winter hymns.

Fiery skies awake darkness deep
colors dance from nighttime sleep
warmer faces tip and glow
witness more than ice and snow.

Rains come down clouds then speak.
Wavelets craw toward each creek;
runaway rivers swirl now free
blessed water returns to sea.

IF I COULD

If I could run my heart on air
I'd press the wind against my chest
and smile rainbows near storms
that give leaves little rest.

If I could guide my soul to earth
hold it there unaware
I'd stand on ground built of stone
barefoot every spring I swear.

If I could teach thoughts the sun
shine a ribbon long and bright
I would walk from shadows dark
holding closely to the light

If I could wander in the rain
cling all wet to other things
I would then know all songs
the body electric sings.

RIVER THOUGHTS

In river thoughts green strings of algae curl and turn
hearts forever waken in streams flow
fingers touch songs on sweet lips
where banks spread wide willingly.
Inside soul birds flutter
wings gifts wind.
All water seeks its own form
frenzy dances verdant hair.
The gods laugh they do!
They laugh I swear!

TODAY I AM

Today I am with you.
I am life you hear singing
moment exploding
love you feel inside of you.
I am bliss with thought and wonder.
I am everywhere you are
holding you
trembling with love
dripping with song.
I am your skin
inside your skin
inside of you.
Everywhere I am
I am your eyes
watching
your yes.

MY MIND IS

my mind is
a whirl
of you
my spirit comes
to you
at this moment
wind in your hair
kisses all over
you
kisses everywhere
yes there
there
and there.
I cannot comprehend
dreams depth

yet I see you

as sea

rocking under me

over me

I into you

you into me

great moment

waves of life

great moment

of free

as we spend

ourselves joyfully.

MY NAME IS TWO DOGS

My name is Two Dogs. I was born where the sun
stops rising and begins to fall. All around me are
trees and wind and stones and rivers
speaking their way. I have come from a journey
long and travel where my moccasins
touch the earth with my face to the sky.
I have no argument with the universe. It is
the screen of my being the hope of my
trust the loss of my heart. I follow the way of white
clouds and the turn of red wind. I speak the voice
of wolves and weep the sound of a woman's hair.
My hands are eyes as much my vision as whisper
lips truth speak. Down by the great sea my thoughts
are pipers darting here and there chasing the surf
pecking sunlight. Love is my great light that

shines even in that depth where all sound disappears.
I have come this way before and I may pass here
again.
If we chance to meet let us speak.
Let us hold this moment in retreat.
Another like it will not come again. It will not repeat.
In this manner we are blessed.
You also have come this way.
Though I do not know you I hold you dear.
I hold you complete.

WALK WHERE WISE WATER FLOWS

Walk where wise water flows
where tumbling whispers dance on stone
where little gurgling moments splash and bubble
wise tug the heart with eagle eyes.
Walk where sun speaks light truth
lover of shadows tears of trees.
Mark your shadow your own pale light
bend to drum heat of night.
Your skin's soul shouts spills and tumbles
your poem's rhythm rumbles rumbles.
Walk where wind tells all laughter
leaves golden and flying sway of pines
toward weather's quest
jump and turn on seasons dying
each lover's moment blessed.

Walk where earth welcomes feet
trance with her explode life.
Kneel down kiss her grasses green
sing her mermaids night.
Whisper that whisper you nearly hear
it is your own soul breaking thought
so prance sing wildly now
or forever lose moments caught.

WHAT WOULD IT BE

What would it be like to hold you in the dark
beside warm wind and palms speaking their way
with waves talking their say along the shore
giving light enough for turtles ocean return?

What would it be like to touch a moment like
this writing loves embrace across your skin
electric glow feeling fingers close yet no
touch your hair dreaming of wind?

What would it be like to know face of sea
where rings of wash turn splash to sand
to ride with you water covering all of us
we move with against water's command?

UNDER THE SALT SEA

It is a moment under the salt sea
a place where only mermaids go
a moment rich and clear
that sounds and images
beating hearts clutch to each
cling like milkweed fuzz making love
on wind before that moment
of journey to space.

MORNINGS AFTER RAIN

Mornings after rain is our gift of water,
bearer of damp love over leaves and grass
time to dance and dance and dance
red sky come and star to hold
wind breath whispers in our chest
walk earth our bare feet down
our laugher lifts our songs a flight.
Mornings after rain so full of love
sing dance breathe such delight.

YOU ARE WHITE FEATHER AT THE RIVER'S EDGE

You are White Feather at river's edge;
I hear your name spoken softly as wind.
We have walked here you and I together tamed
our passion while moonlight fell across
our blanket shared. Coyotes tell us their story
not so much different from ours
not so different from great earth arms
holding us here in her love
our holding her and each in ours.
Everywhere is your smile
your hands in your eyes
your heart in your hair
little songs dance across your lips
my own close enough to feel your singing.
I am in your love dark place forever

you welcome me there and my gift to you.
Though we are both merely dream
swimming in thought watching in wonder
our waking hours we must know
what is was what was is
what we are we are always.

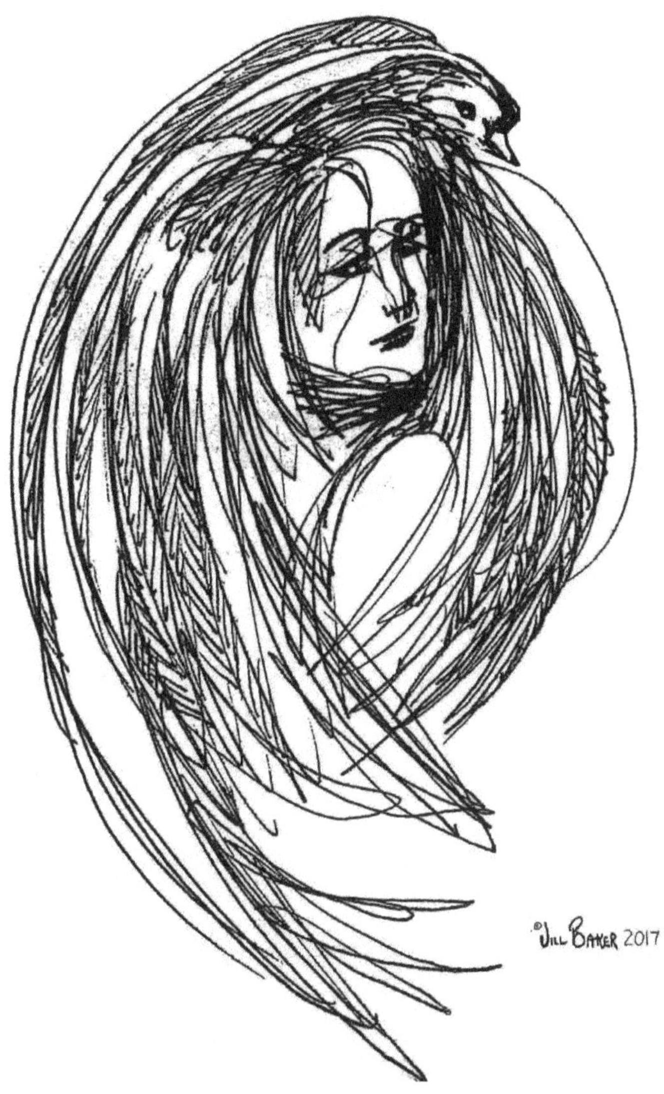

White Feather

WAKE EACH DAY IN WONDER

Let light come slowly into your heart.
Let wind whisper to your face
although you're listening to moon.
Hold in your heart rushing waters
mountain streams tumbling
singing full their songs.
Let earth's heartbeat be your heartbeat
your heartbeat be the earth's.
In one great moment stand by sea
watch double sun
one in sky one in waves;
watch her tumble toward you.
Stand where she falls mirrors the sand
feel water's breath around you
make it your breath.
Be in that moment all you are
all you can ever be you at once
light water wind earth and sea

I CANNOT CONTROL WIND AND RAIN

I cannot control wind and rain.
I am no match for sun or night.
I hold to earth by hour in holy turn
cling only to moments relish each.
When pretty party plates fly by
I only watch then only reach
for birch to sway from earth to sky
I dream and wonder and plan why
yet perhaps it does not matter much.
I hold to truth where it is found
I try to hear her call and clutch
the great white cloud best as I can
though sometimes not at all.
In many instances I wander by
the purest dark and all
I cannot escape songs in flight
having heard mermaids call.

I COULD

I could hold you close as ice
but choose what light has sent
to wrap your silent falling hair
in all of loves intent

I could speak a welcome wind
talk to lovely trees
or move with care behind shadows
of flying honey bees.

I could be your river dance
splash you all around
I could jump the tallest banks
to your highest ground.

I could be your gift of earth
dark and loamy true
where roots find their magic
in your morning dew

or I could merely watch your heart
beat its feisty way
perhaps hold you close enough
to hear what mermaids say.

I TURN TO WORDS

I turn to words when singing spreads her wings
takes me through a glass bearing love
fly to welcome dreams living things.

Words have little feet that run and play
my thoughts themselves motion's gifts
never knowing what they're going to say.

They're little broken sticks washing down a stream
catching here and there on rocks rough edge banks
water voices and light never exactly what they seem.

They come in herds sometimes stampede
roundup of love of time of place of you
bunches of little critters wildly to be freed.

SONGS ARE NOT TO BE SUNG BUT EATEN

Songs are not to be sung but eaten like prize
rose petals on tongue melted tight
juicy thoughts dripping butterflies
word music swells with wisdom right
moments deep in kisses one time wise
tender long wild birds warm in flight
milk wonder bliss commands the skies
melody surrounds rapture of night
dark active dances filled with fireflies
blinking tastes of loves delight.

I GUESS I AM

I guess I am a waterfall tumbling over cliffs in spray
of wonder questioning not rocks below but loving
sound the oh so precious sound of giant splash
runaway waters perfect scream I guess I am river
stream
turbulent and bent spread yet smooth wide and deep
turning grass toward the sea changing aim of beavers
swim pointed toward distant shores clutching limbs
ships their own in muddy swirl tails banging flat a
water clap
I guess I am wind waking green tips of limbs rising
to dance the startled light of morning come
touching flowers laughing and screaming under feet
of bees their little wings wiping pollen across the face

of love I guess I am swirling clouds carrying rain
above
my hair songs of sirens gleam their eyes everywhere
I guess I am the earth breathing universes delight
one hand holds the deepest dark the other the lightest
light.

LEE PENNINGTON

Lee Pennington has published 20 books, most of them poetry, as he is a Poet Laureate of Kentucky. B.A.--Berea College, Berea, KY, M.A.--University of Iowa, Iowa City, IA, DLL--Academy of Southern Arts and Letters, Doctor of Lit. (Honorary)--World University, Danzig, NY

Pennington, who grew up in Greenup County, Kentucky, is the author of nine other books of poetry including: *Scenes from a Southern Road, April Poems, Songs of Bloody Harlan, I Knew a Woman* and *Thigmotropism*.

Appalachian Newground was released in April of 2017 and was entered for nomination for the Pulitzer by the publisher. This was Pennington's third nomination for the prize in poetry as his *I Knew a Woman* and *Thigmotropism* were previously nominated for the Pulitzer in 1977 and 1993.

After graduating from high school, Pennington attended Berea College and went on to graduate school at the University of Iowa.

In 1984, State Legislature named him the Poet Laureate of Kentucky.

Pennington was a professor of English at the University of Kentucky Jefferson Community College, teaching creative writing and English for 34 years until he retired in 1999. He also taught at several other schools and universities including poetry at the Jesse Stuart Creative Writing Workshop at Murray State University for 10 summers.

BOOKS BY LEE PENNINGTON

The Dark Hills of Jesse Stuart (criticism), 1967

Scenes from a Southern Road (poetry), 1969

Poems and Prints (poetry), 1969

Wildflower Poems for Joy (poetry), 1970

April Poems (poetry), 1971

Appalachia, My Sorrow (drama), 1971

Songs of Blood Harlan (poetry), 1975

Spring of Violets (poetry), 1976

Coalmine (drama), 1976

The Porch (drama), 1976

The Spirit of Poor Fork (drama), 1976

I Knew a Woman (poetry), 1977

Ragweed (drama), 1980

The Janus Collection (poetry/photography), 1982

Foxwind (drama), 1984

Appalachian Quartet (drama), 1984

The Scotian Women (drama), 1984

Thigmotropism (poetry), 1993

Appalachian Newground (poetry), 2016

Daughters of Leda (poetry), 2017

To order more books by mail from the Publisher,
write to:
Winchester Cottage Print
211 Daisy Lane
Louisville, Kentucky 40243